COLORING FUN!
Coloring Book

Coloring

Nowadays, people are finding out that the simple activity of coloring may actually help in calming tension and relieving stress.

Just like grandma's old school, old fashioned cold remedy of chicken soup ...somehow coloring seems to work!

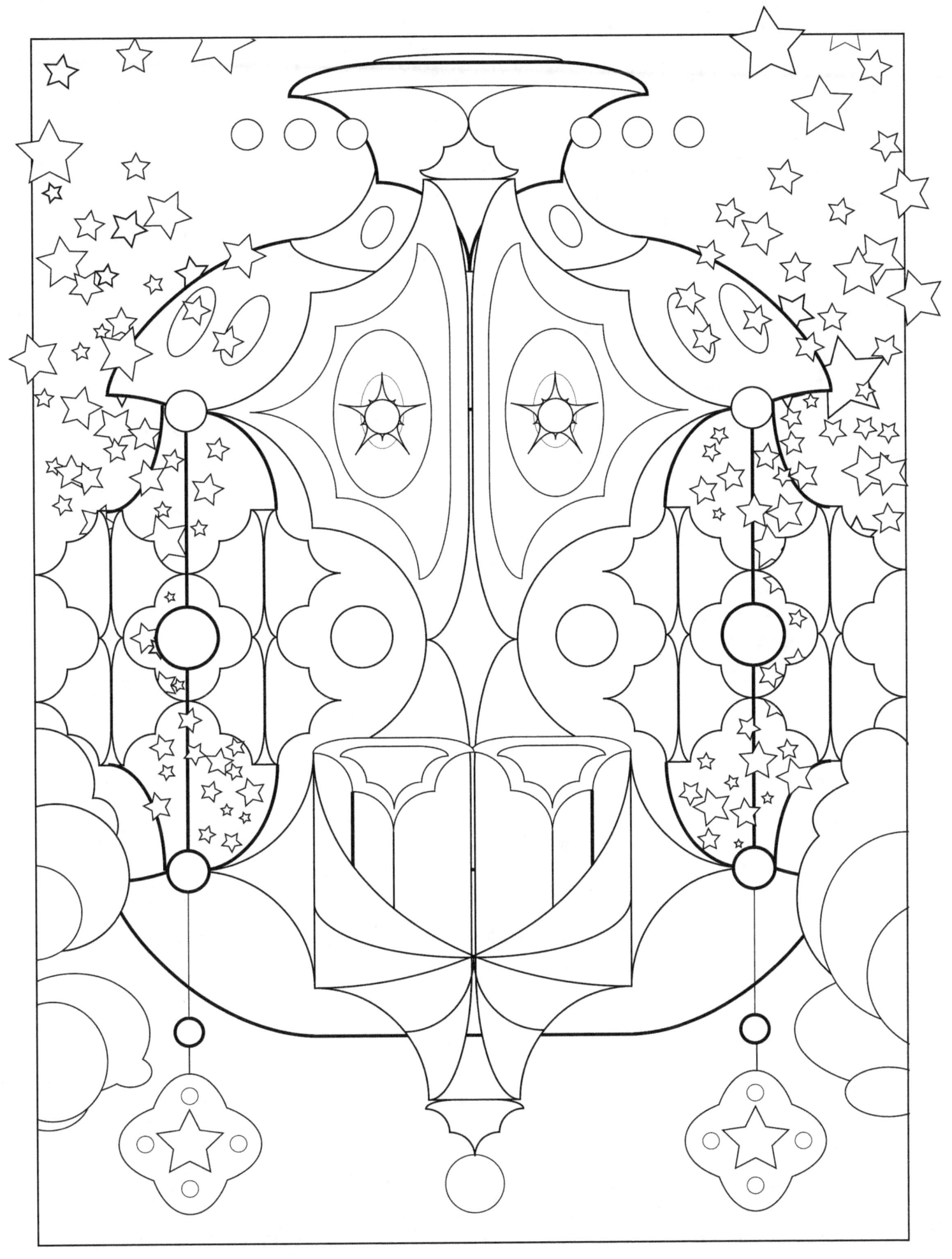

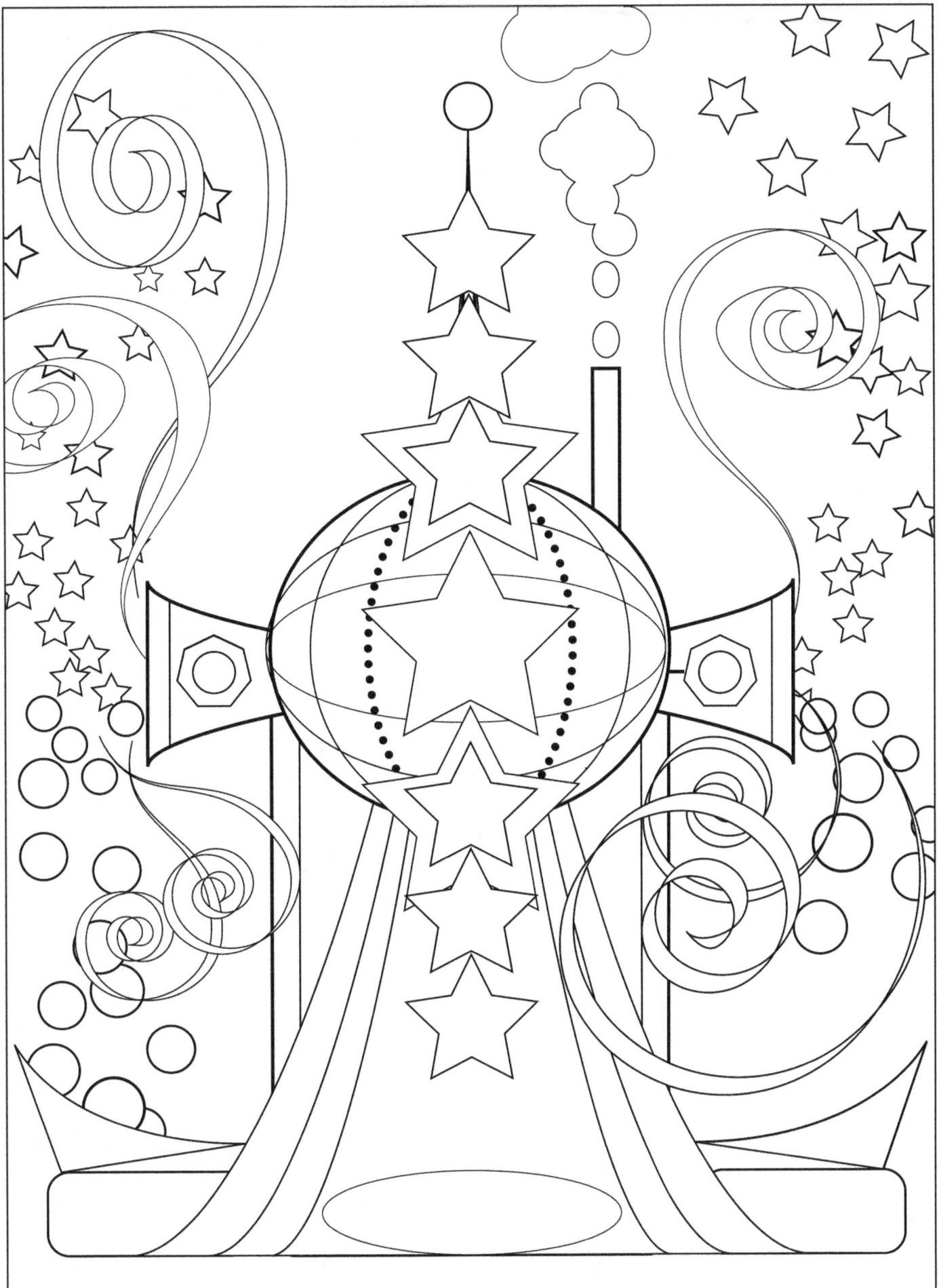

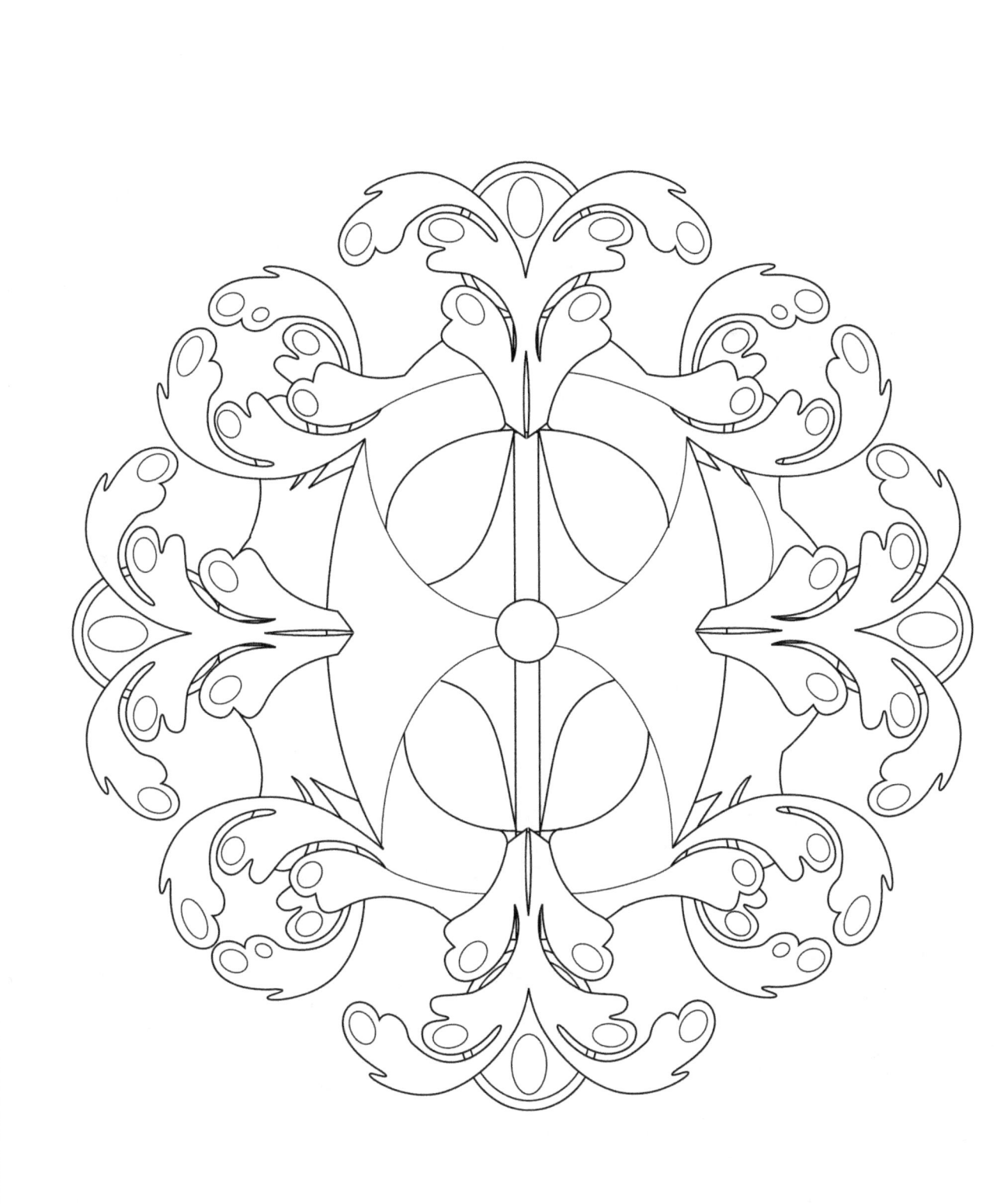

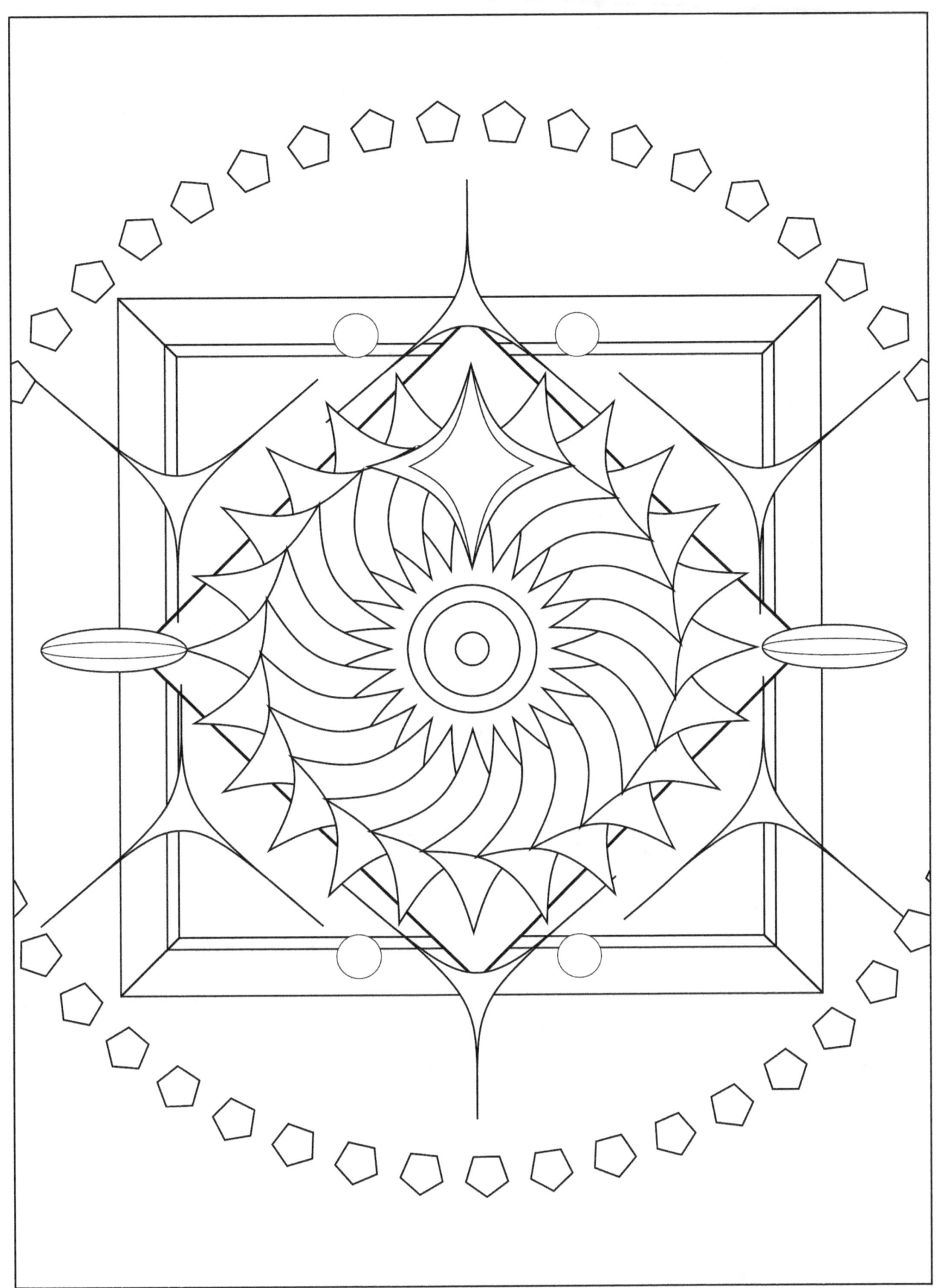

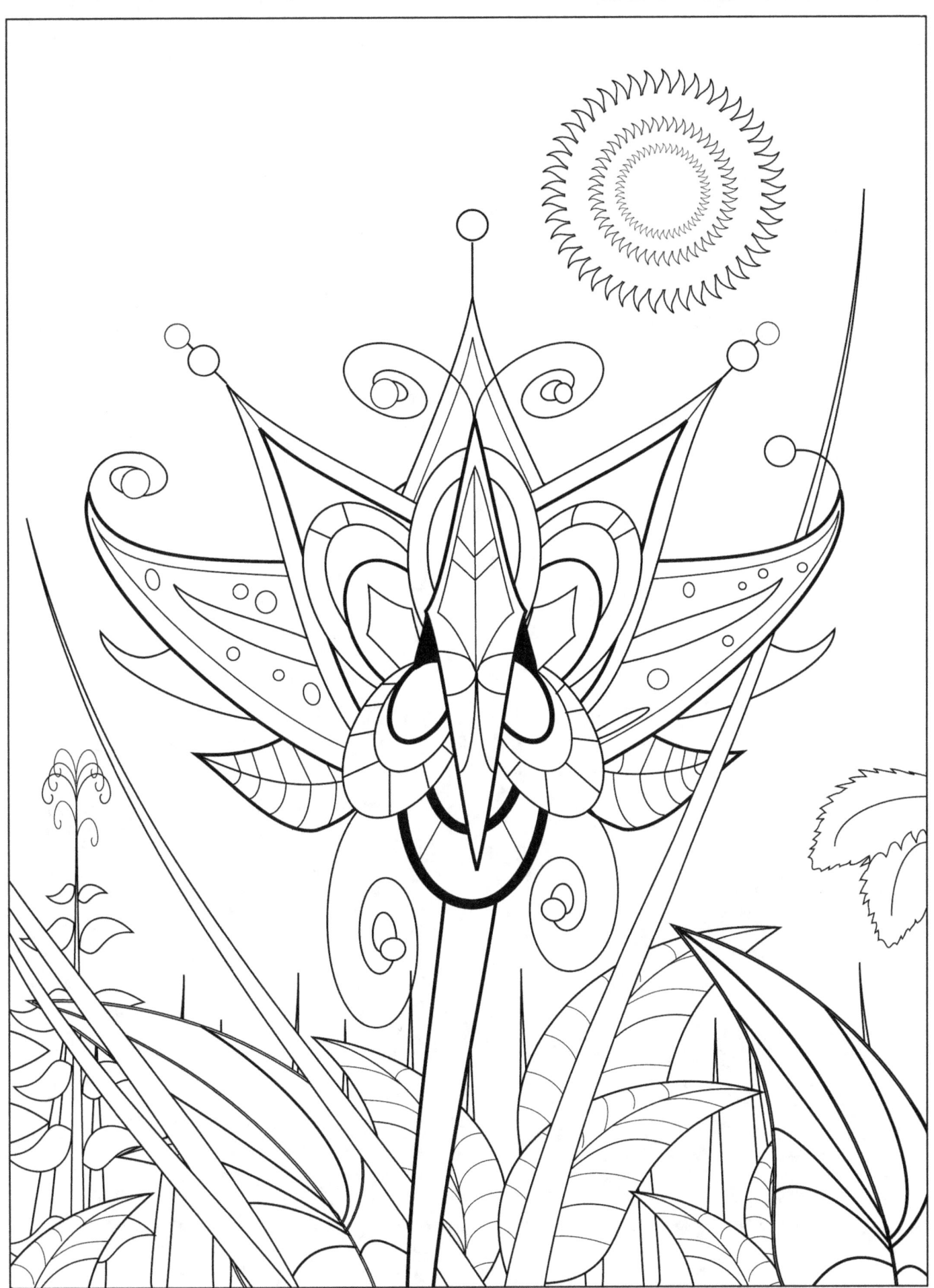

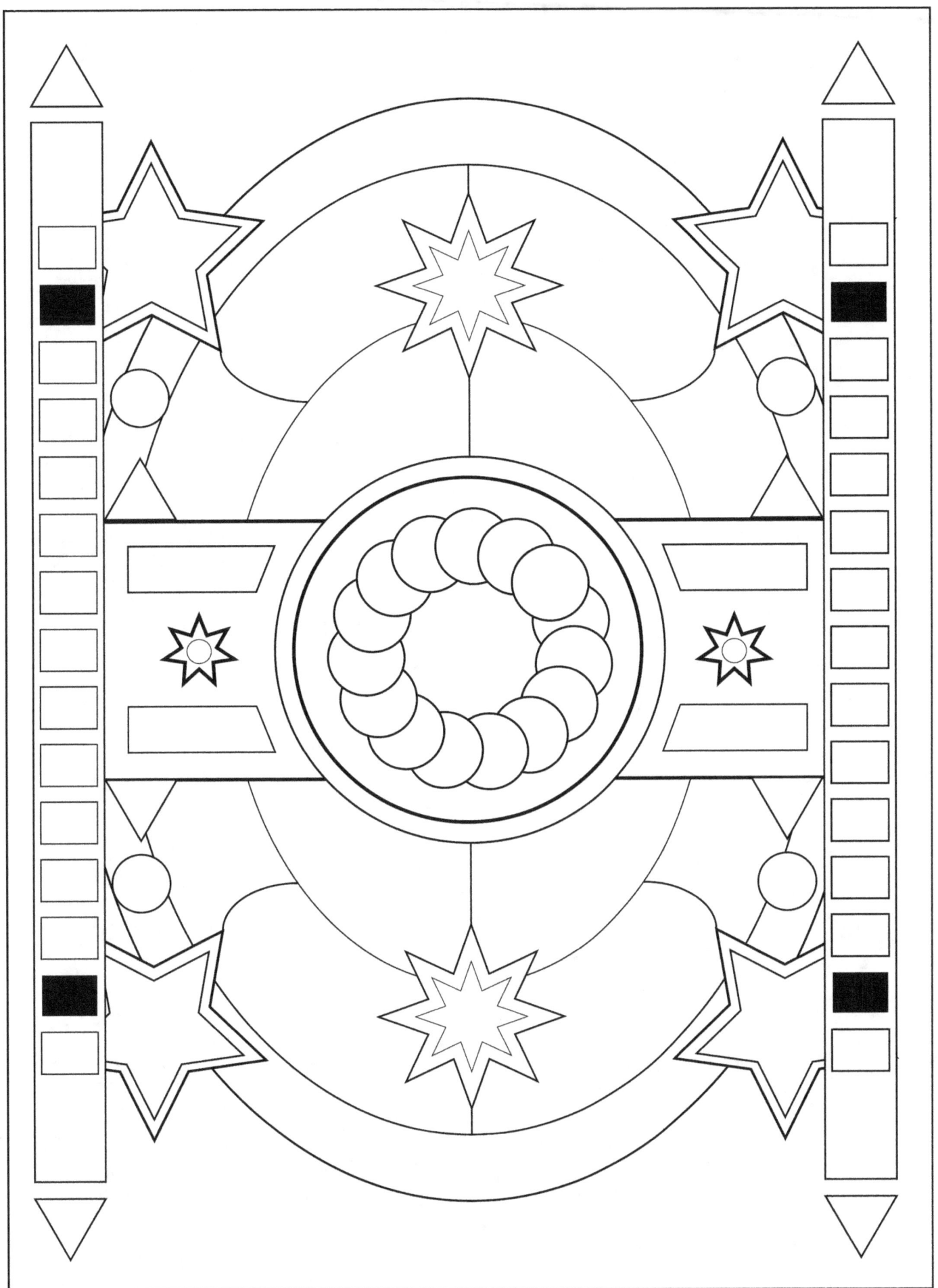

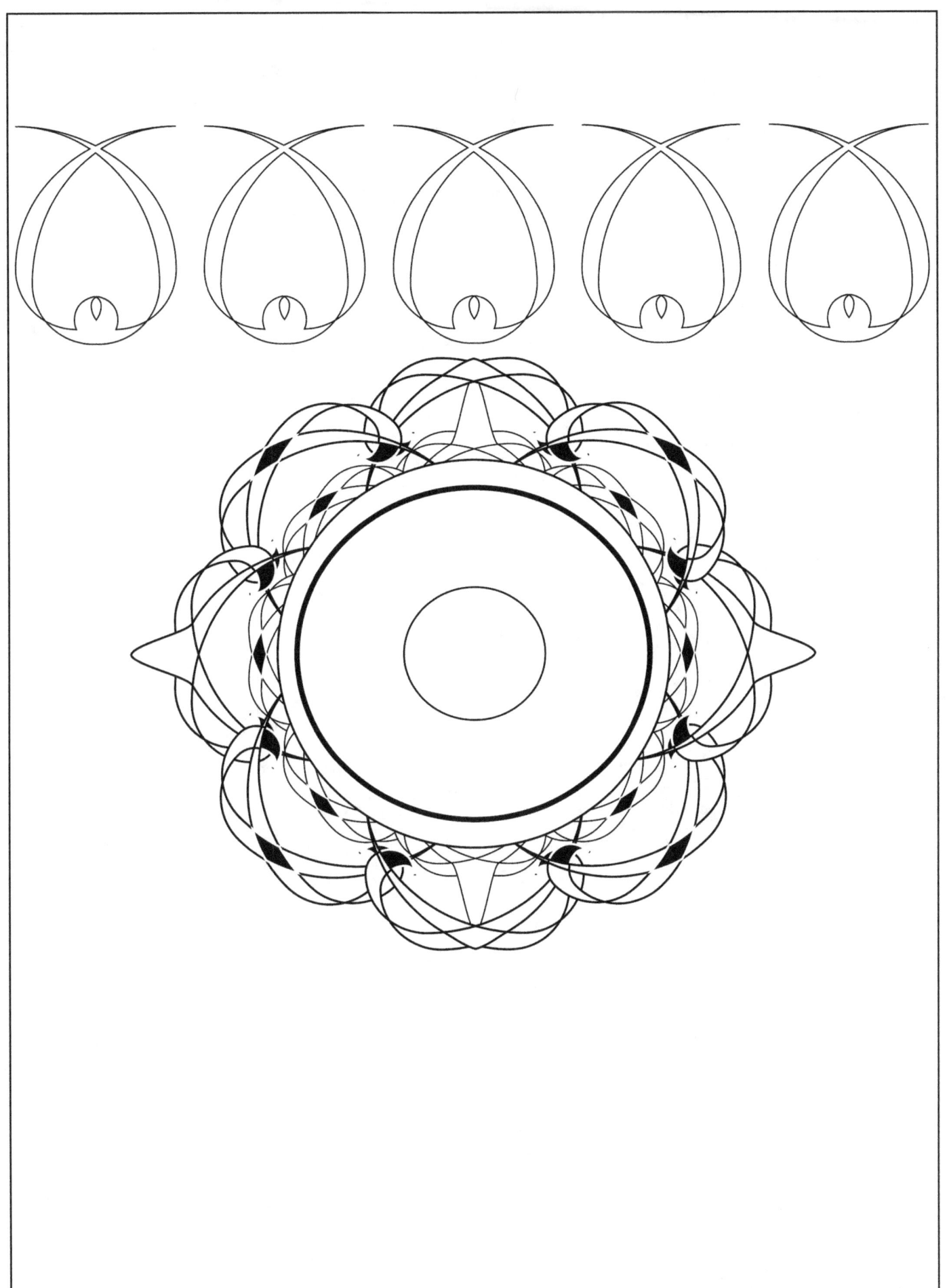

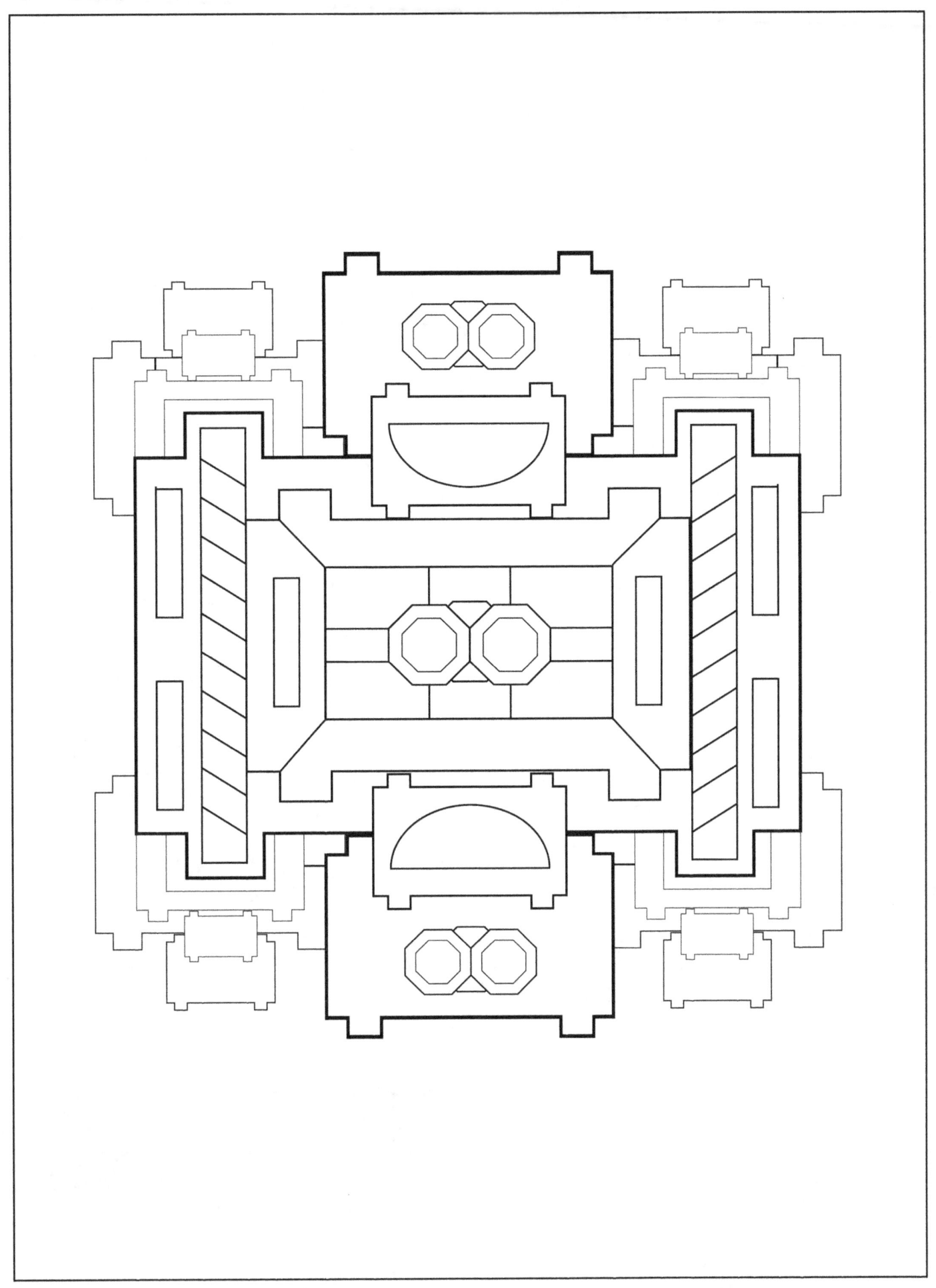

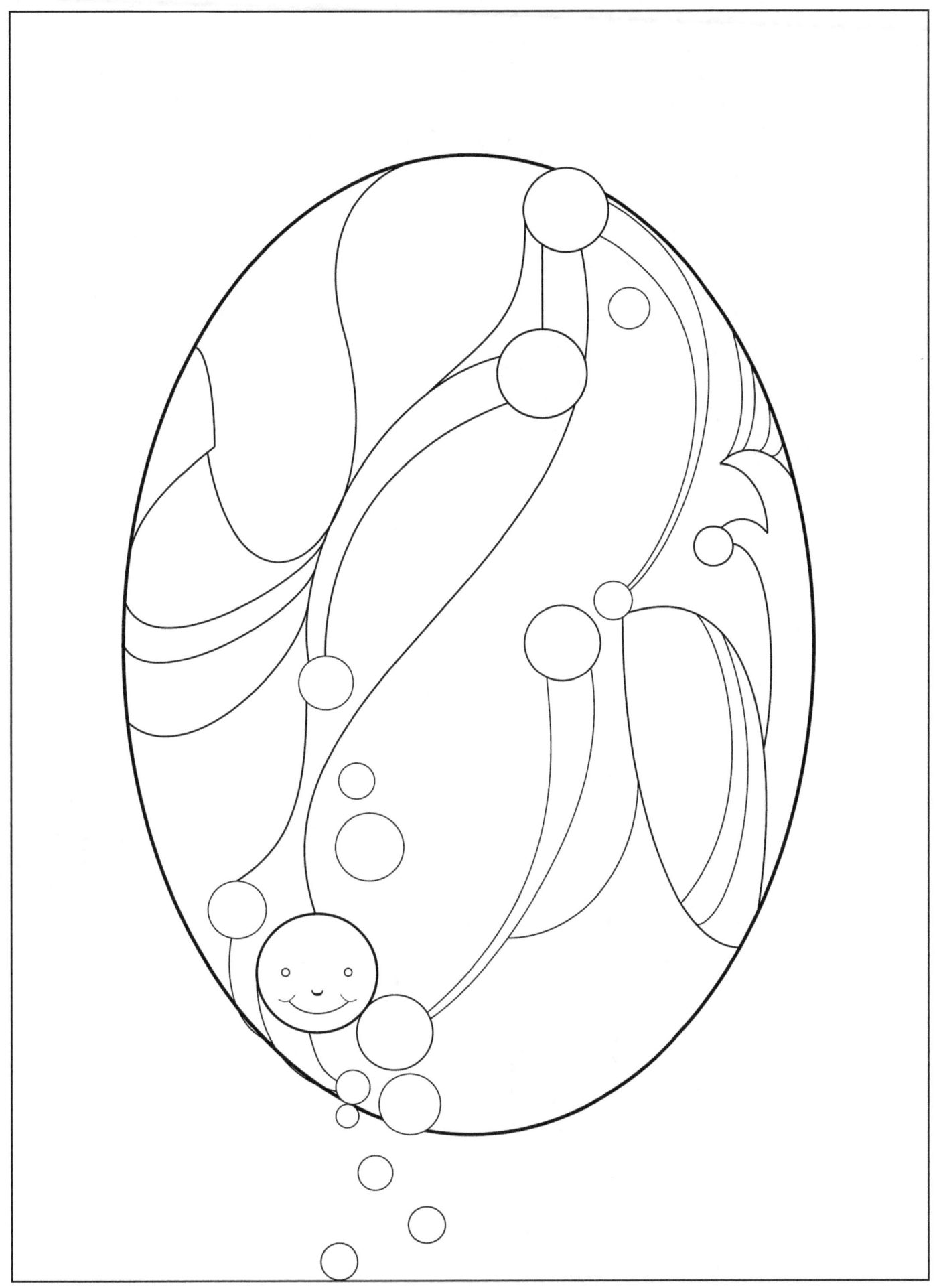

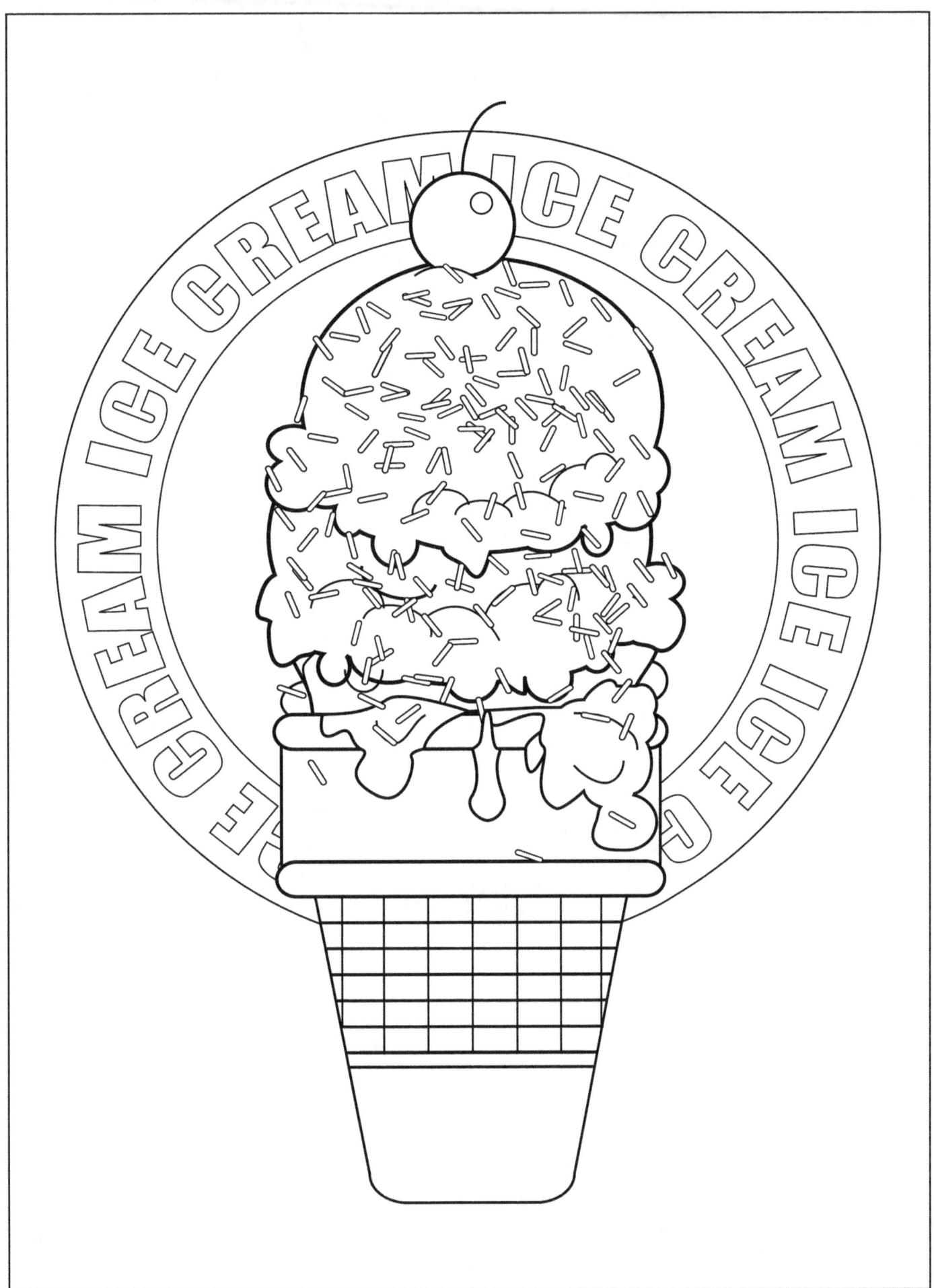

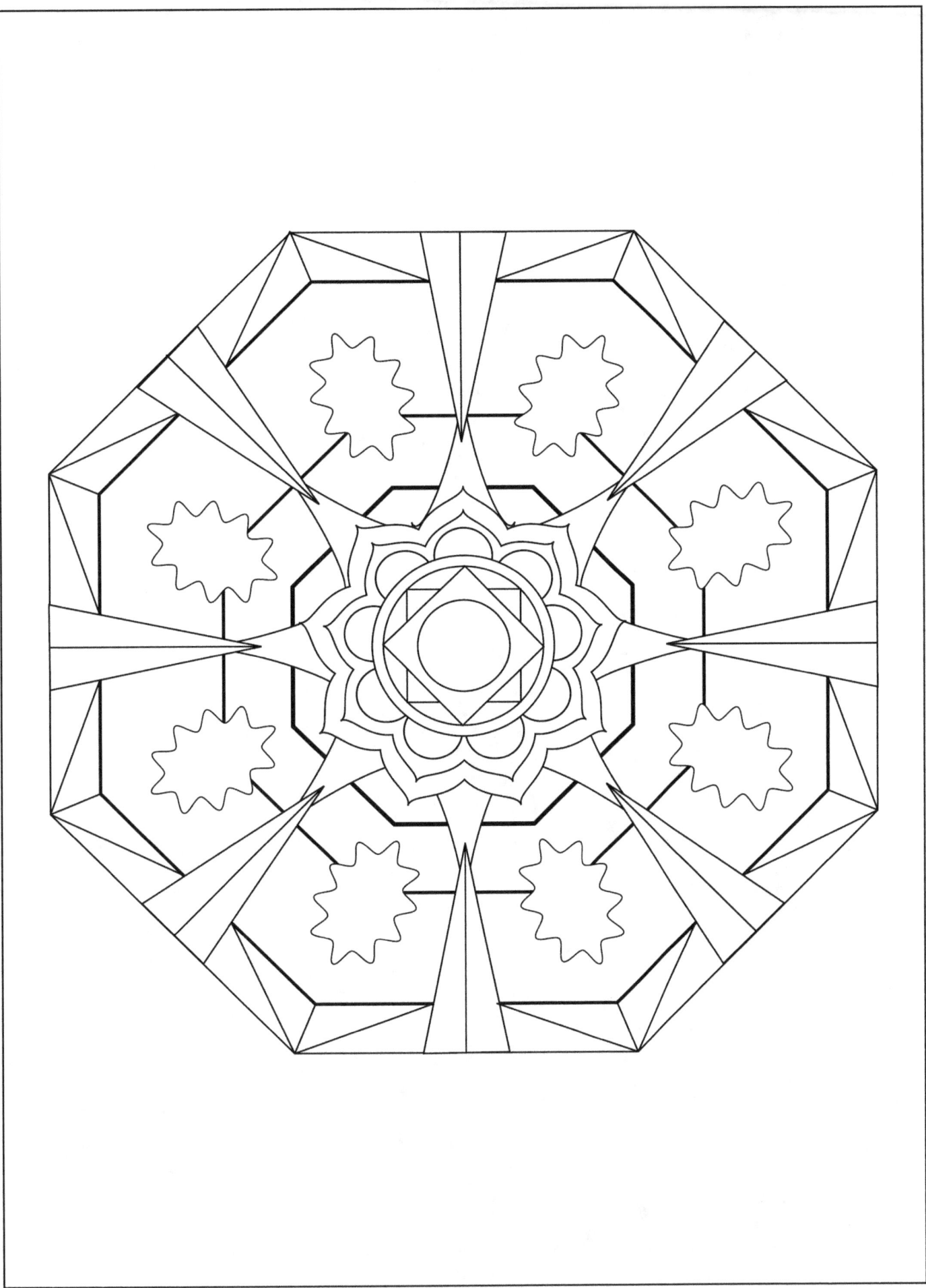

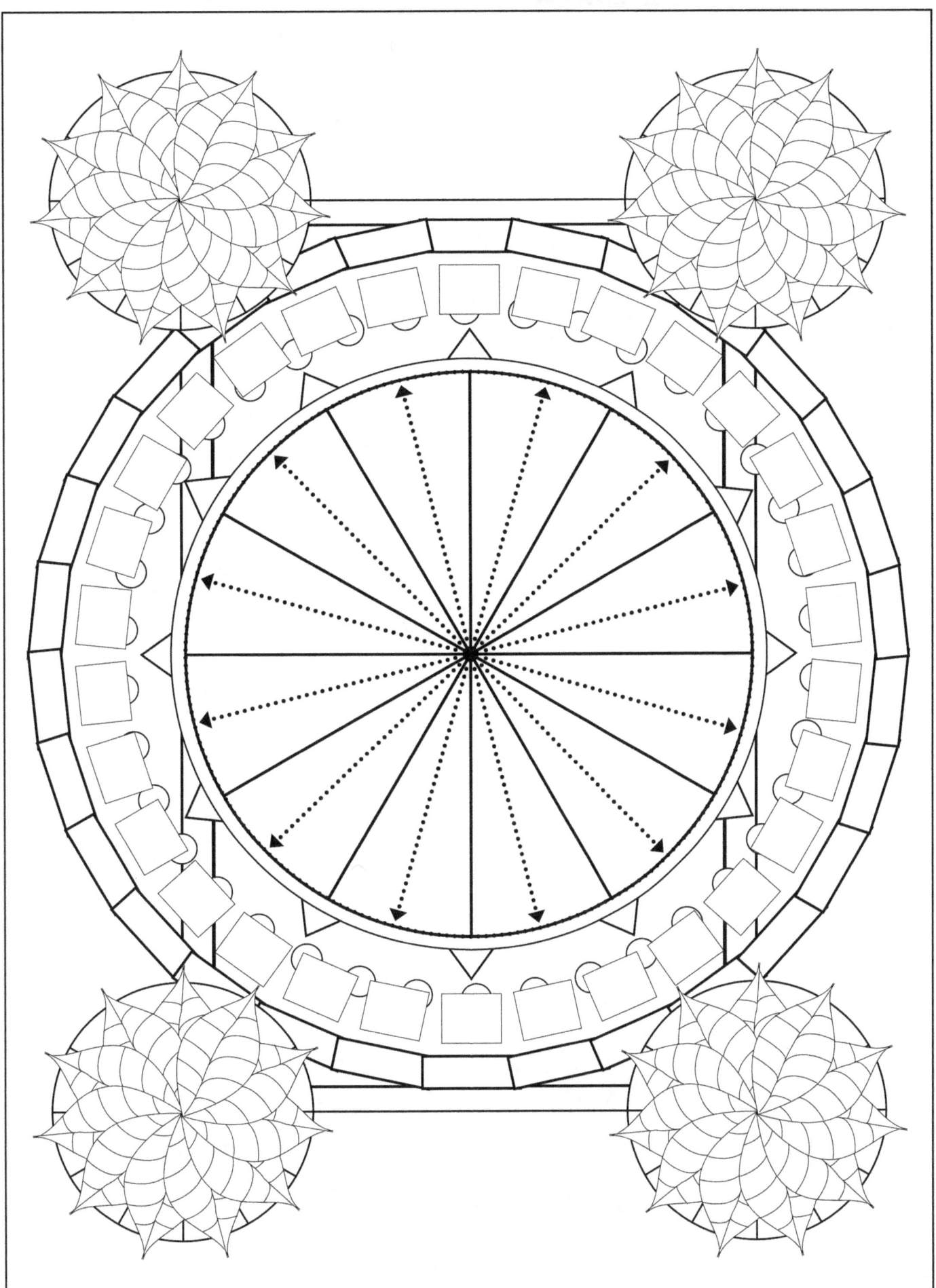

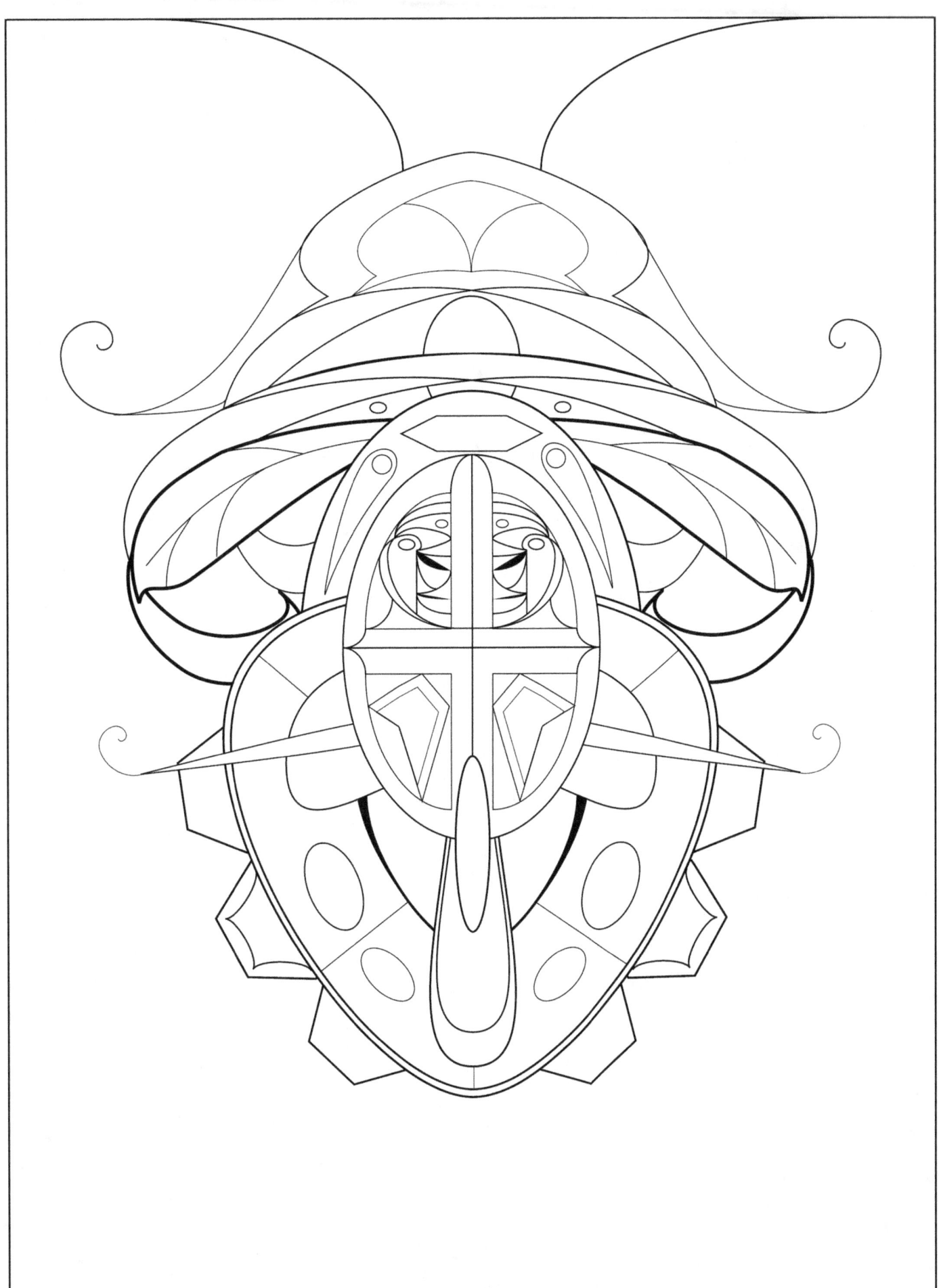

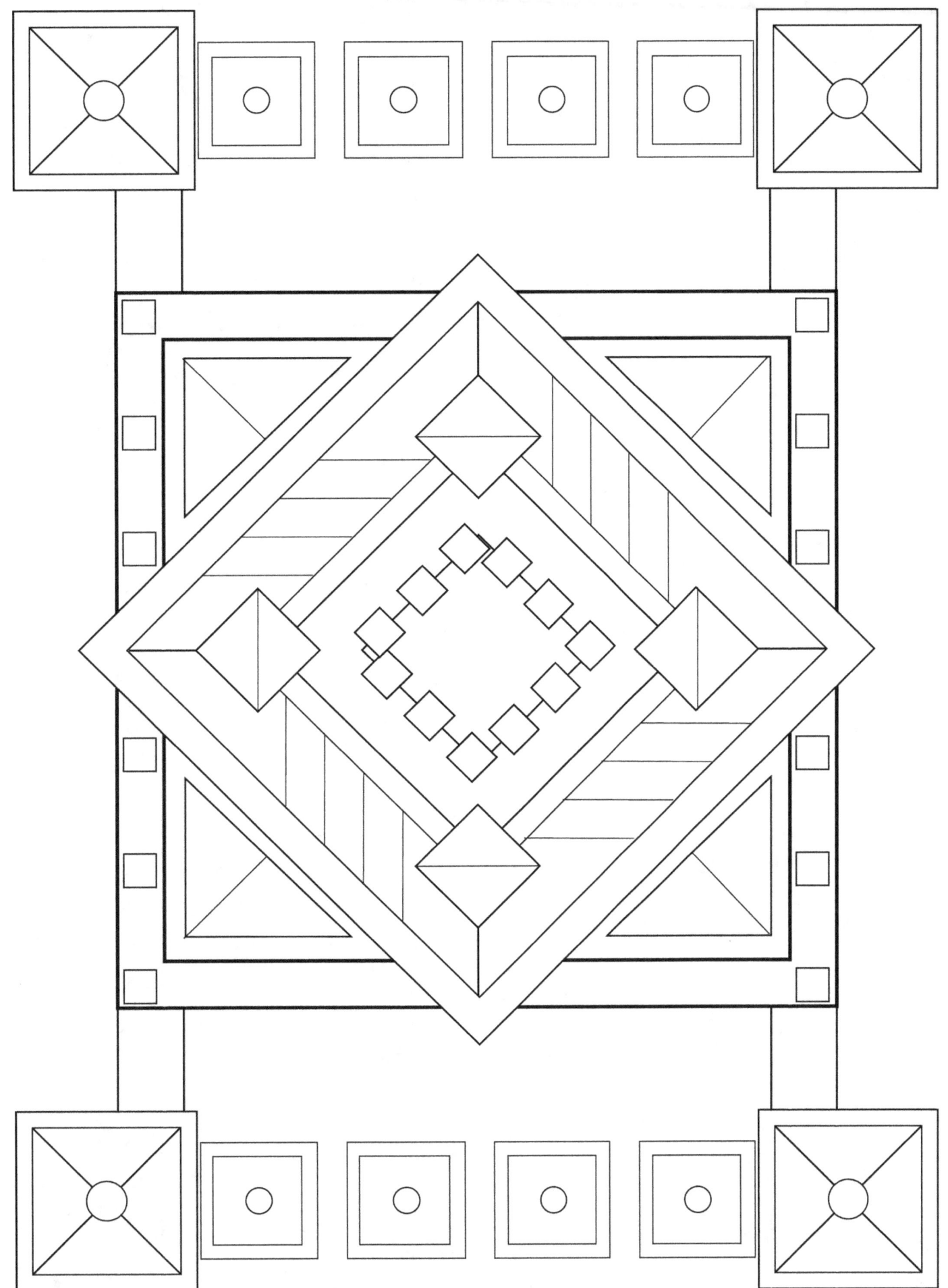

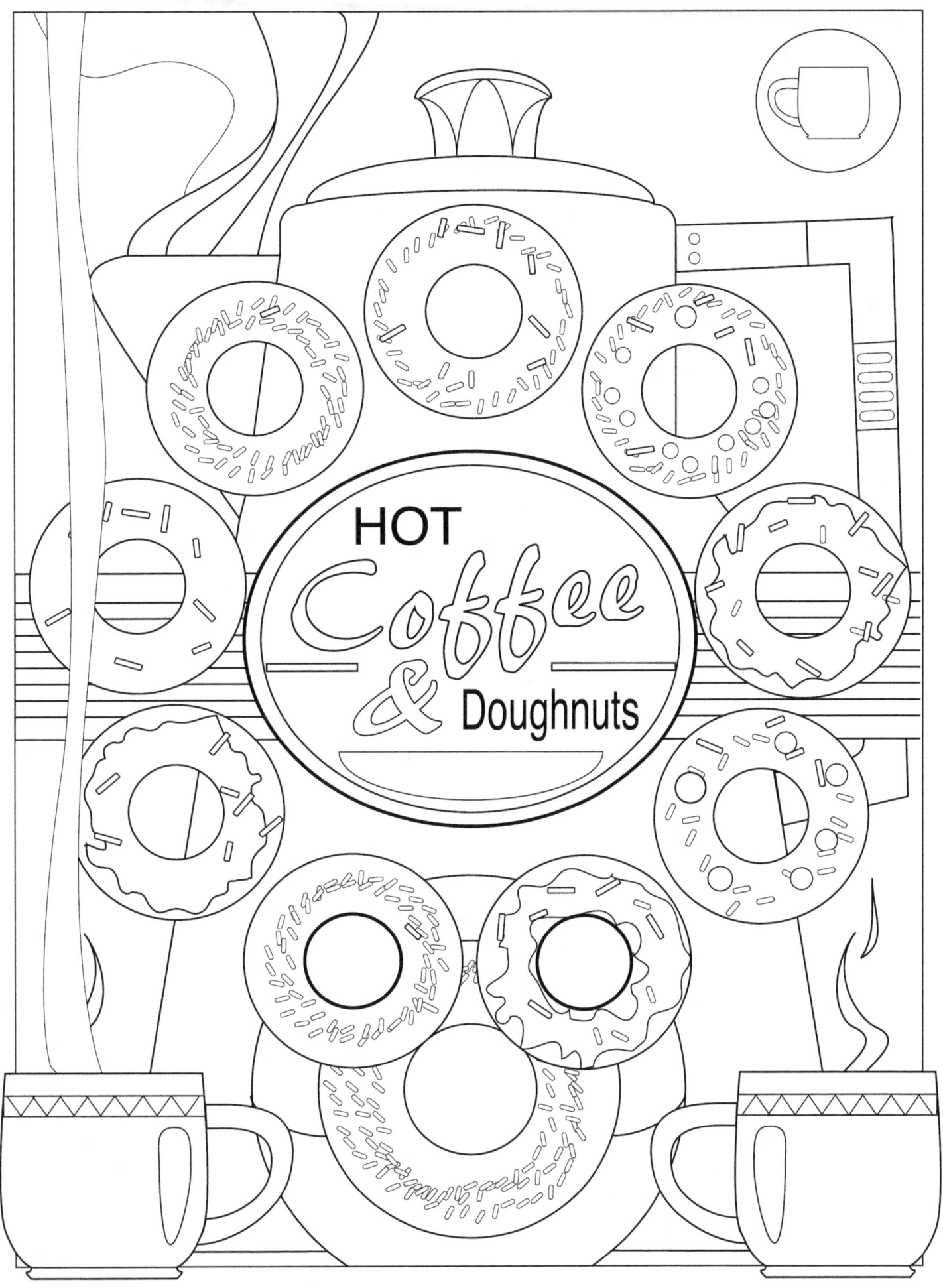

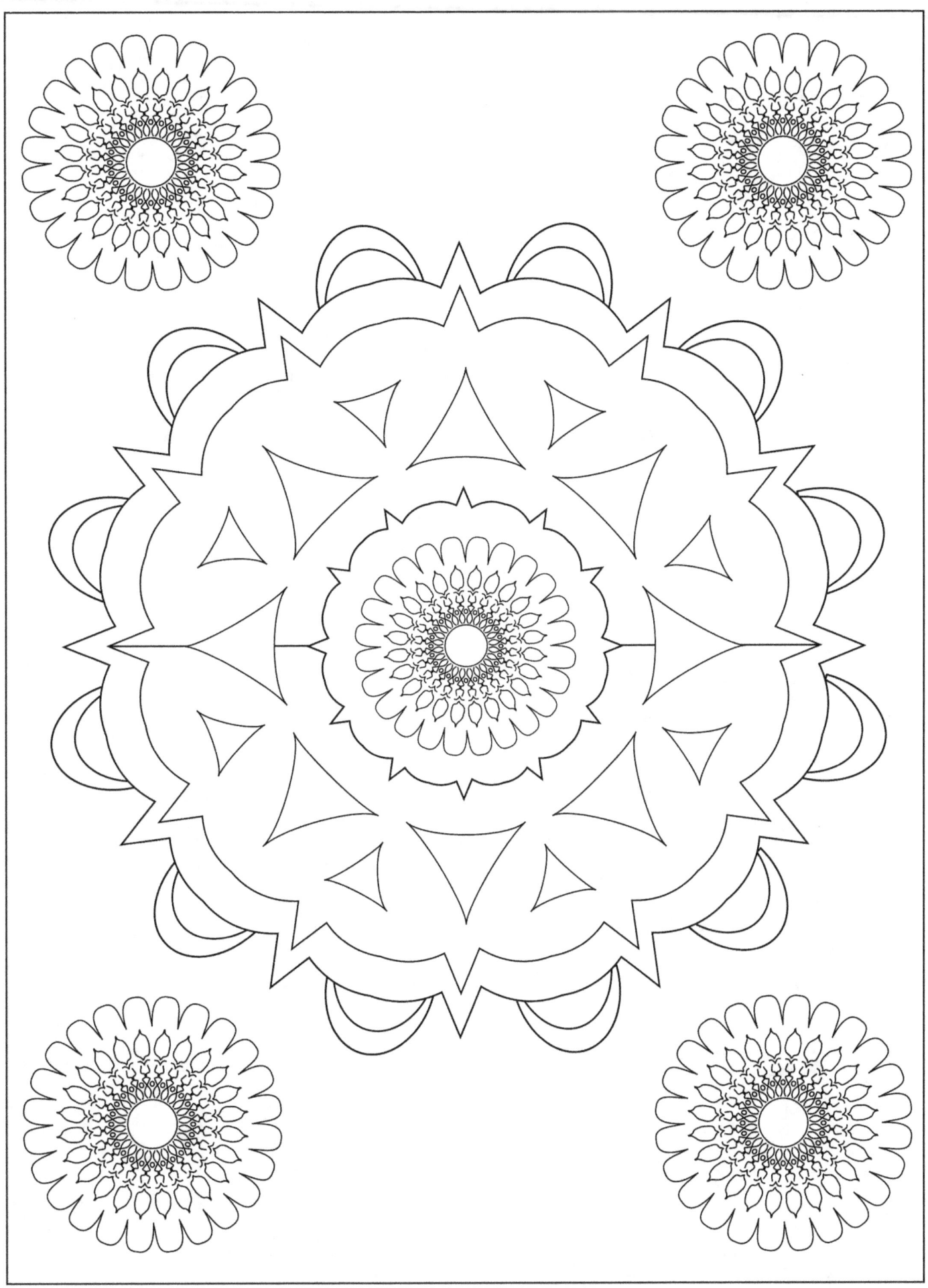

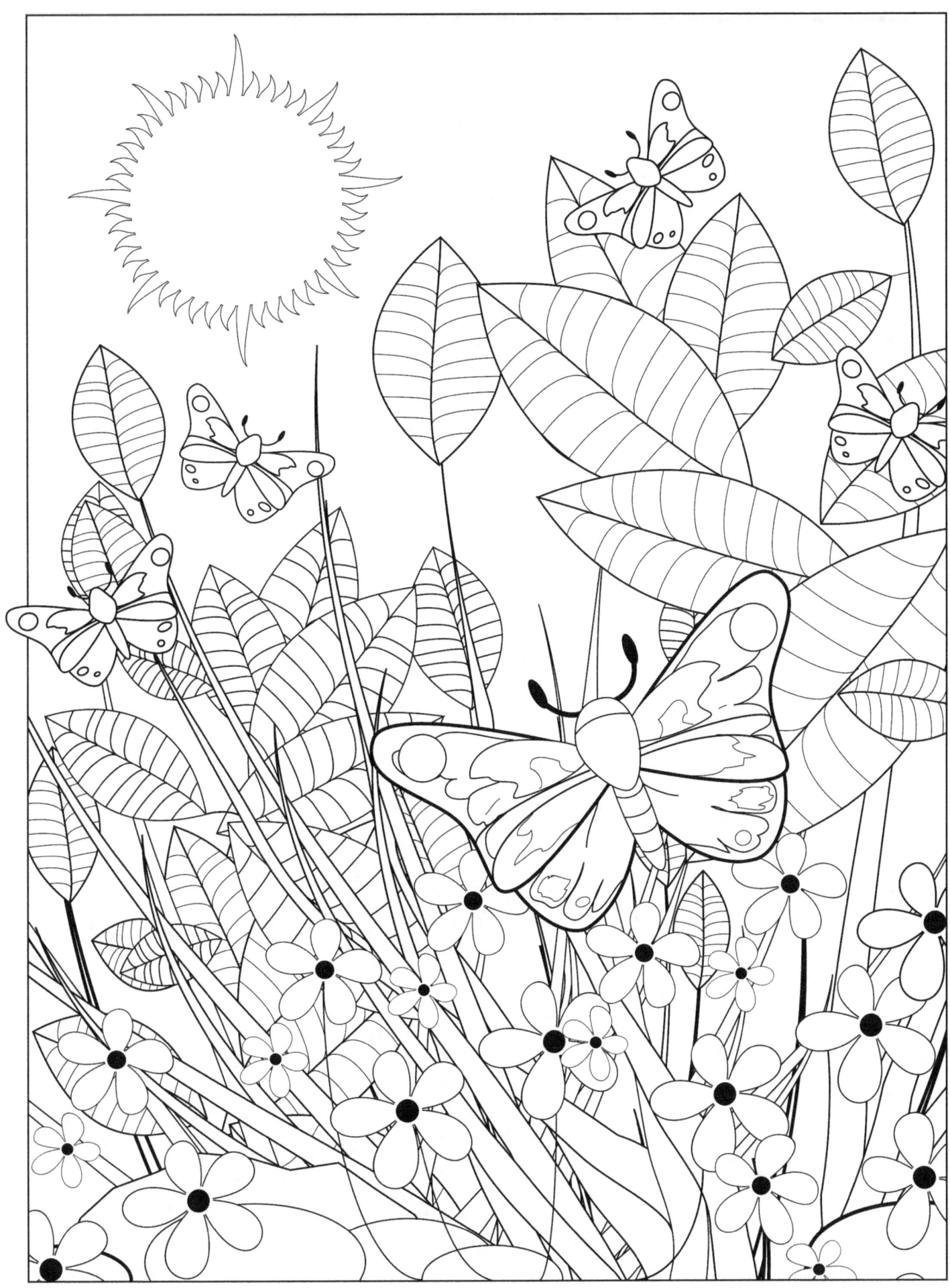

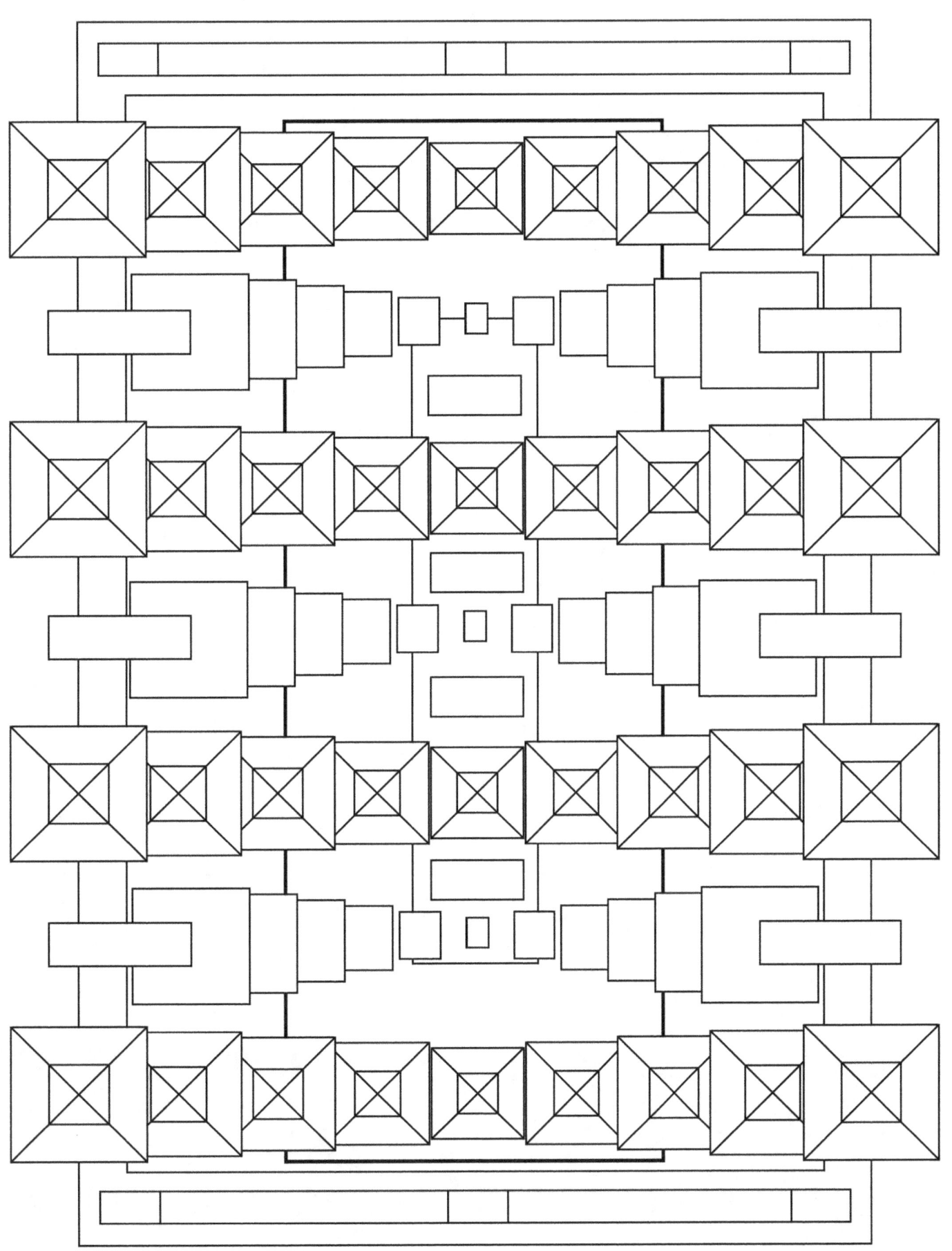

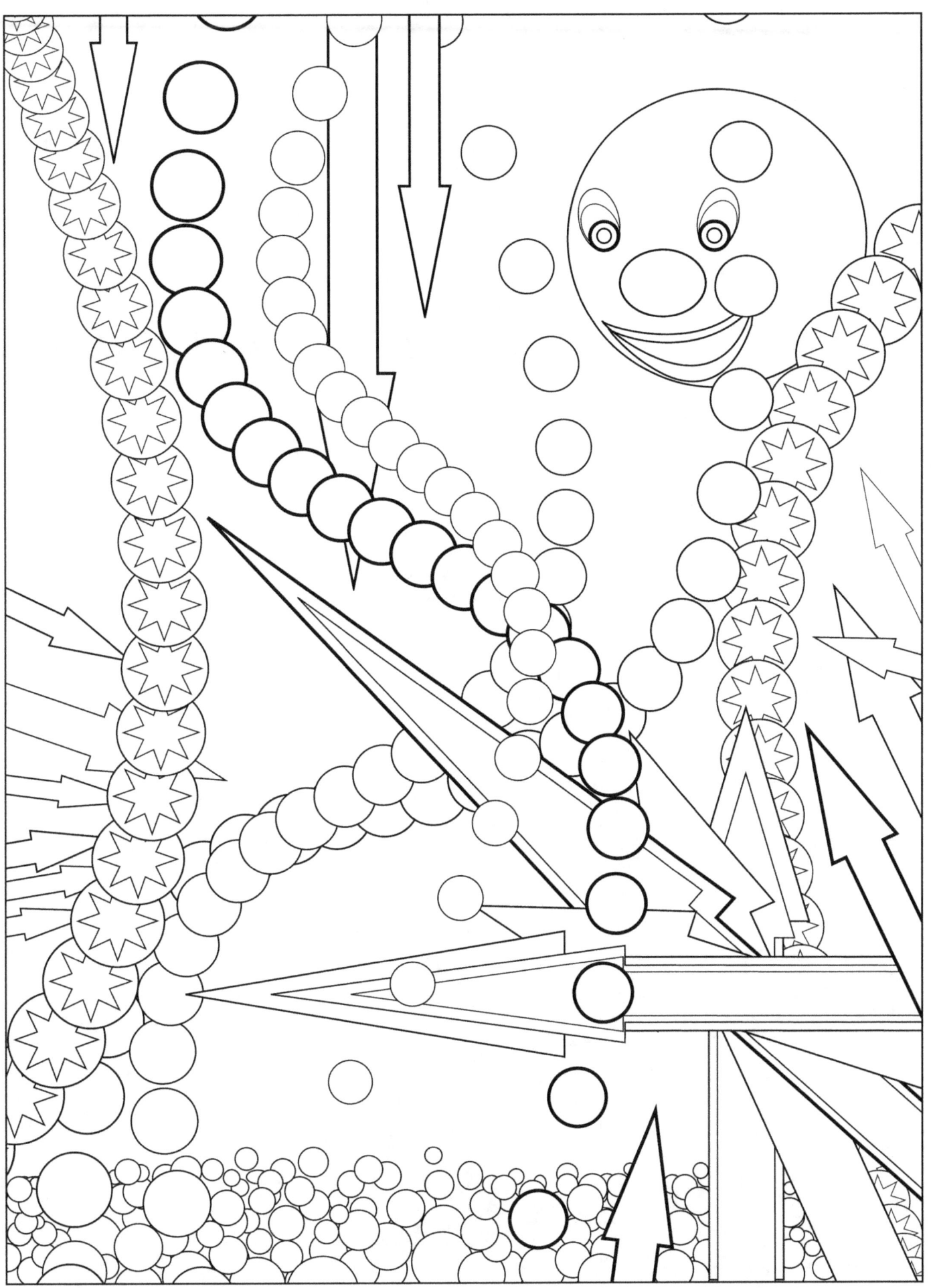

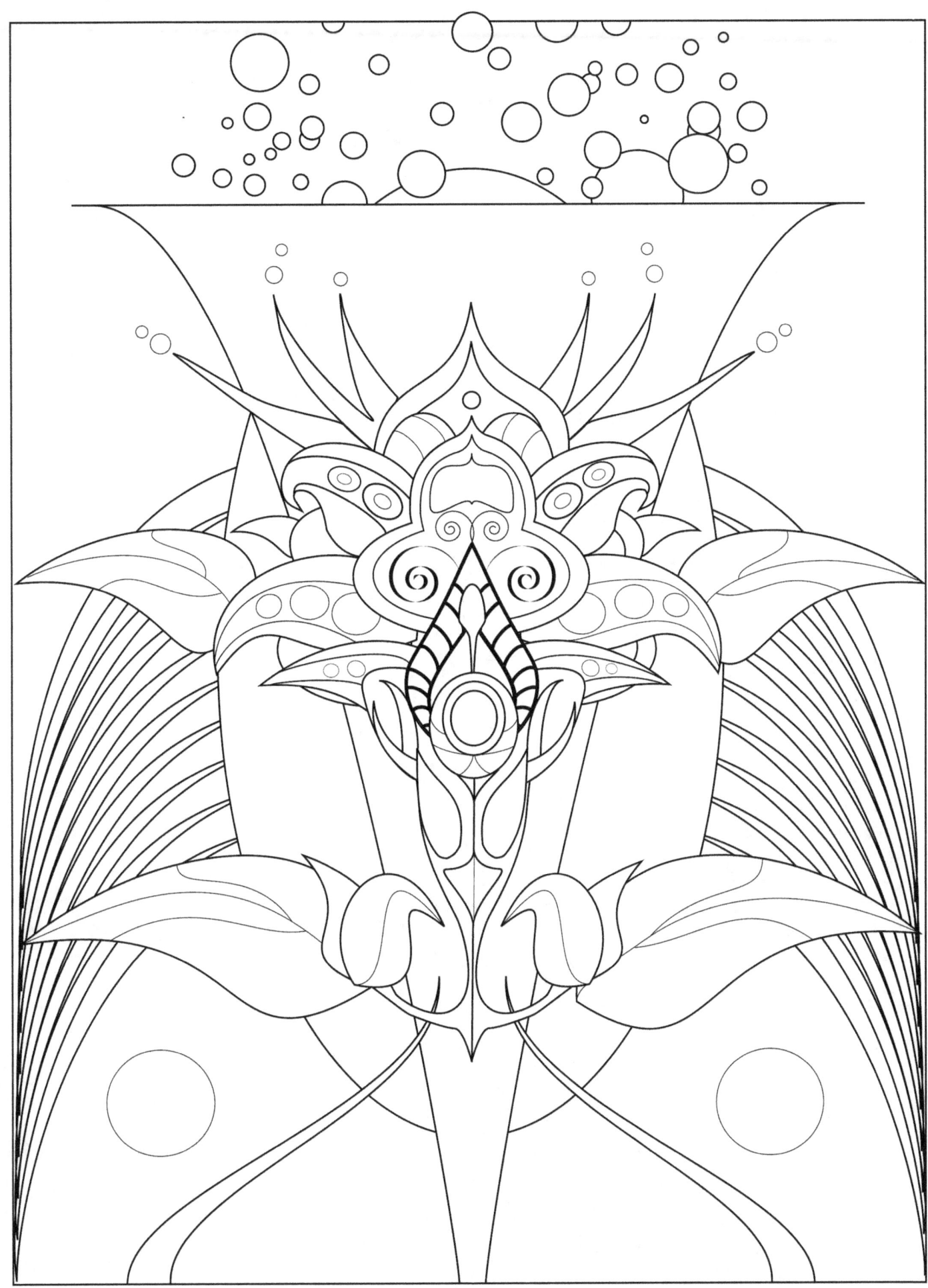

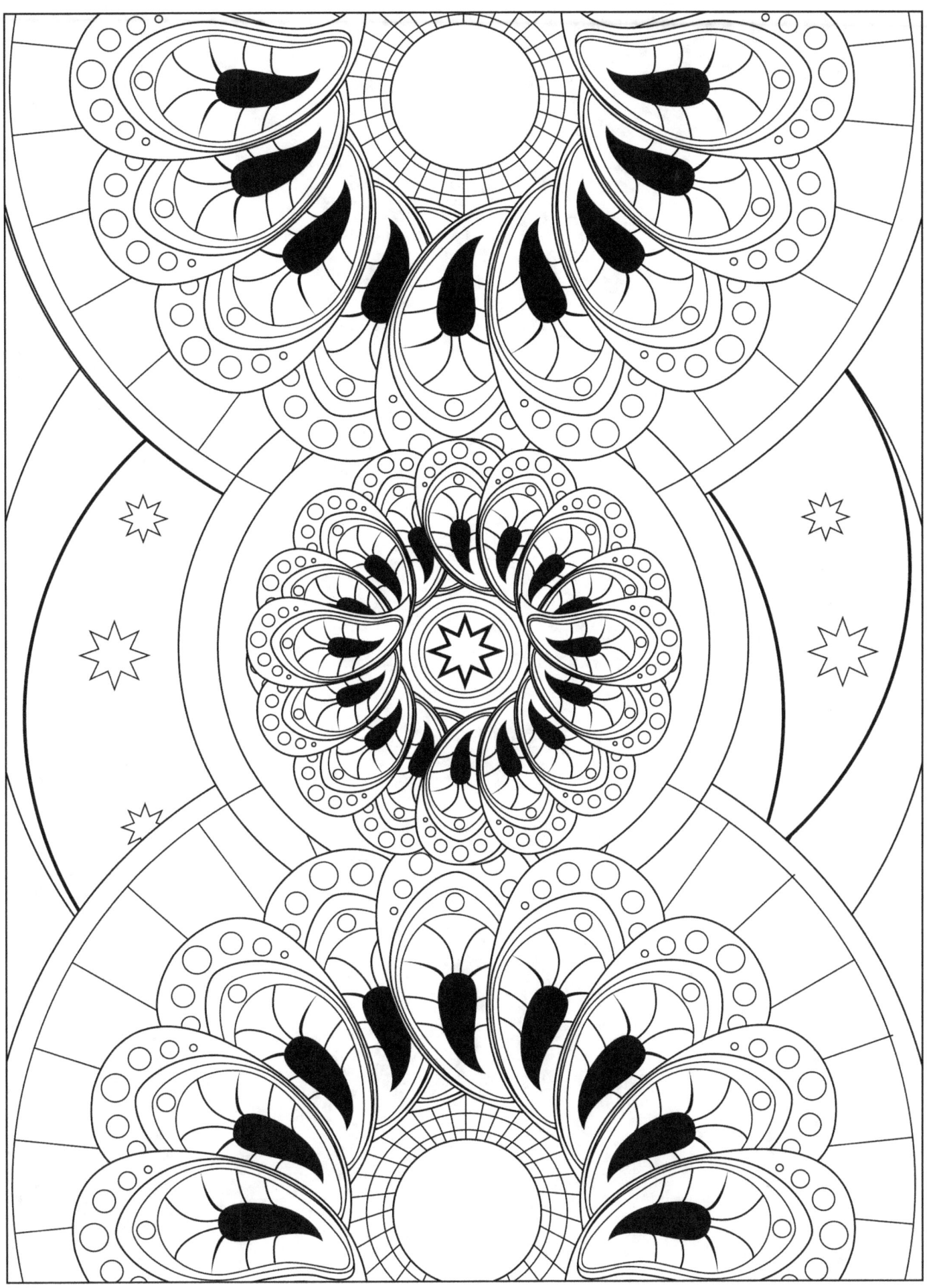

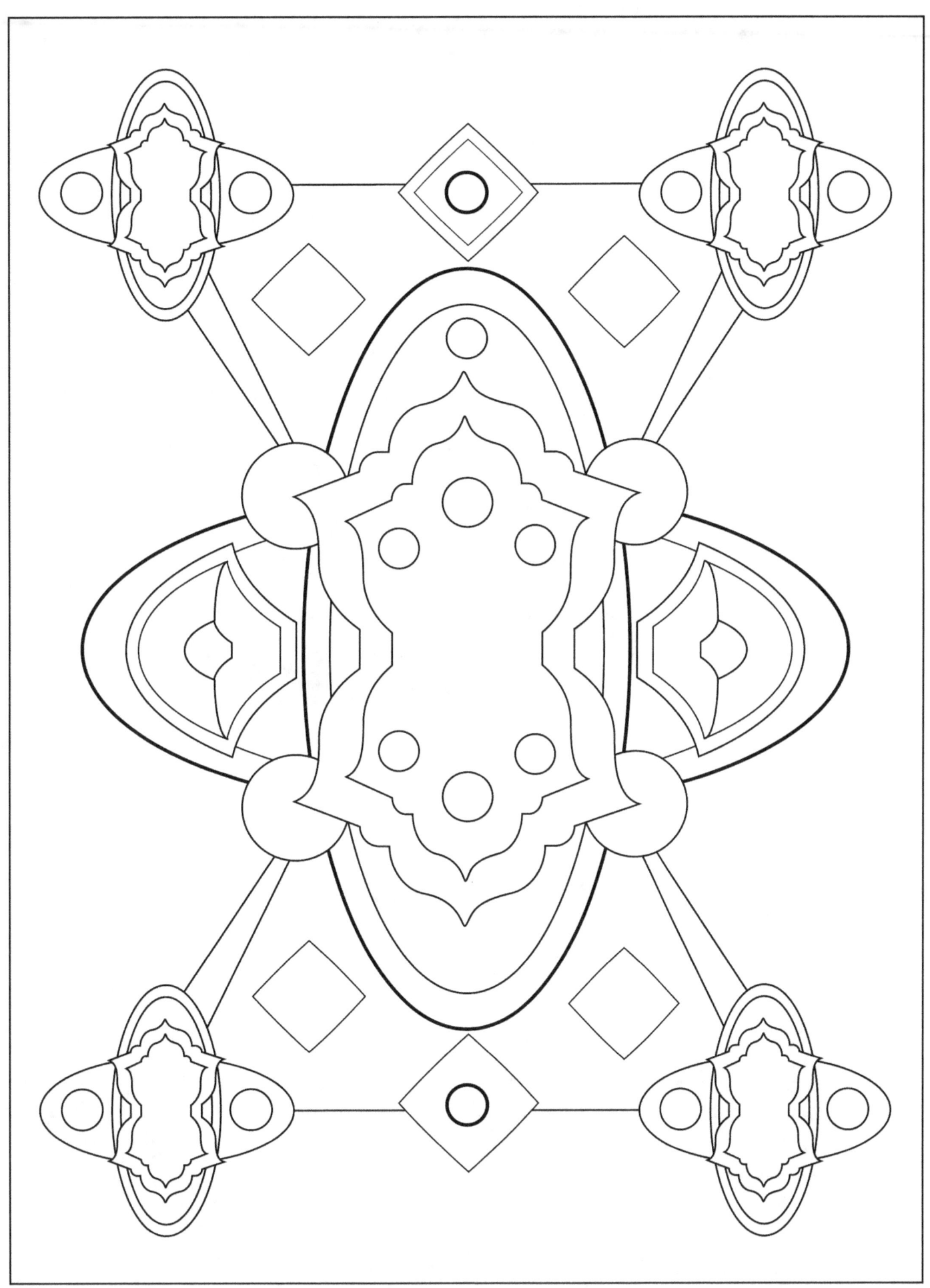

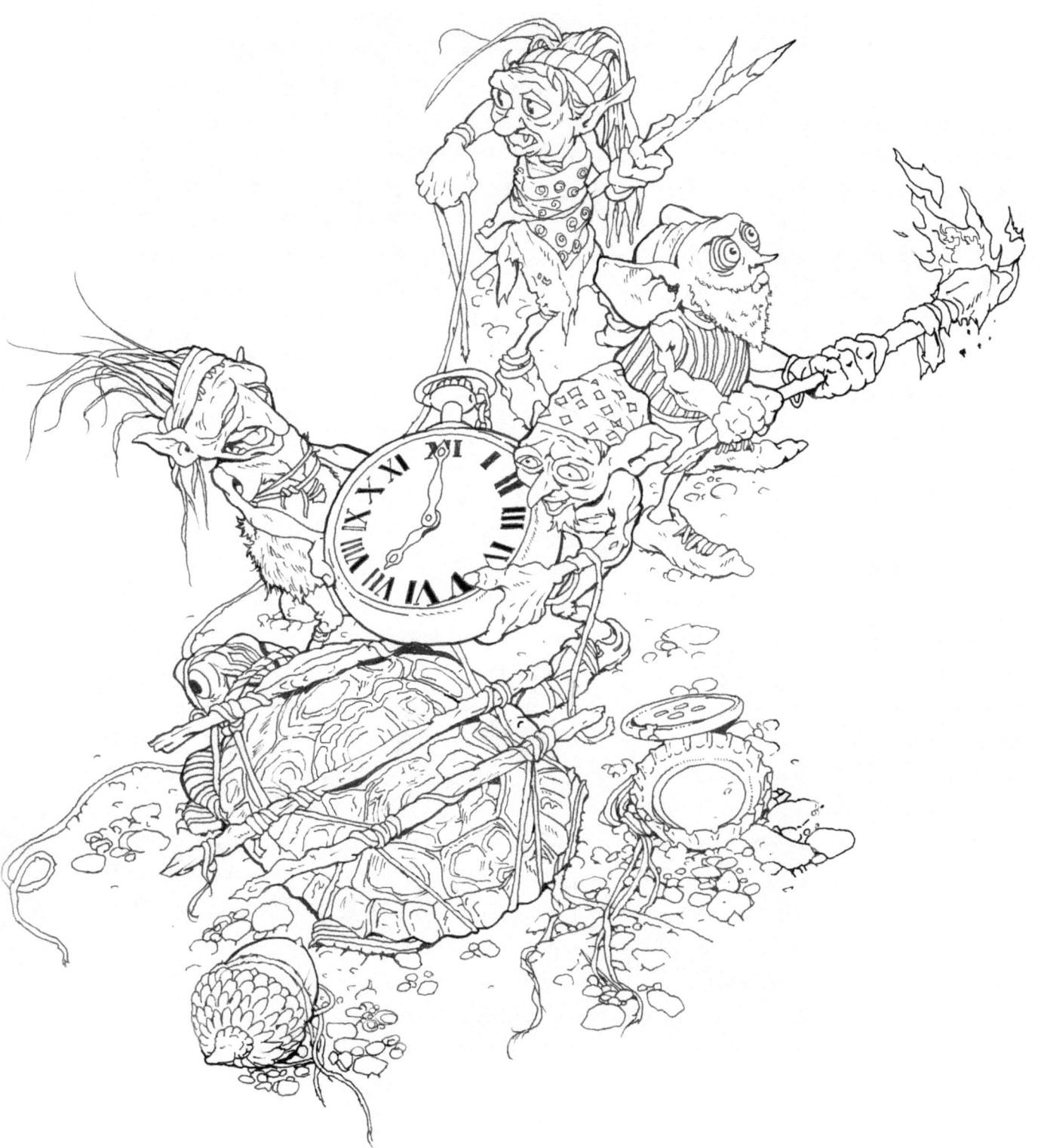

This Scene is from the Tynese Elves coloring book also by Jim Fitzgerald